Healthy Eating

Sylvia Goulding

CHERRYTREE
BOOKS

Published in 2006 by The Evans Publishing Group
2A Portman Mansions
Chiltern Steet
London W1U 6NR

British Library Cataloguing in Publication Data

Goulding, Sylvia
  Healthy eating. - (Healthy kids)
  1.Nutrition - Juvenile literature
  I.Title
  613.2

ISBN-10 paperback:	1842343149
ISBN-13 paperback:	9781842343142
ISBN-10 hardback:	1842344080
ISBN-13 hardback:	9781842344088

PHOTOGRAPHIC CREDITS
Cover: **The Brown Reference Group plc:** Edward Allwright
Title page: **The Brown Reference Group plc:** Edward Allwright
The Brown Reference Group plc: Edward Allwright 3, 4, 11, 16,
18, 20, 22, 24; **Corbis:** 6, 12, 26; **Hemera Photo Objects:** 7, 8, 9,
11, 12, 13, 19, 23, 27; **RubberBall:** 10, 14, 28; **Simon Farnhell:** 4, 5,
8, 9, 11, 13, 17, 18, 19, 21, 23, 25.

FOR THE EVANS PUBLISHING GROUP

Editor: *Louise John*
Production: *Jenny Mulvanny*
Design: *D. R. ink*
Consultant: *Dr. Julia Dalton BM DCH*

FOR THE BROWN REFERENCE GROUP PLC

Art Editor: **Norma Martin**
Managing Editor: **Bridget Giles**

With thanks to models **Natalie Allwright, India Celeste
Aloysius, Molly and Nene Camara, Daniel Charles,
Abbie Davies, Isabella Farnhell, Georgia Gallant,
Connor Thorpe, and Joshua Tolley**

Important note: Healthy Kids *encourages
readers to actively pursue good health
for life. All information in* **Healthy Kids** *is for
educational purposes only. For specific
and personal medical advice, diagnoses,
treatment and exercise and diet advice,
consult your doctor.*

Some words are shown in bold, **like this.** You can find out
what they mean by looking in the glossary on page 30.

Contents

yum yum yum yum yum yum yum yum yum yum yum yum yum yum

Why do we...
Eat and drink?

▼ *Sharing a meal with your friends is good fun. Why not organise a picnic?*

We eat because we are hungry and we drink because we are thirsty. We need food and water to survive. Food makes us strong and fit. It gives us energy to play and work. It keeps us warm when it's cold. It refreshes us when it's hot. Food can stop you becoming ill, and it can even make you feel happy.

Just amazing!

People eat the strangest things...
- Some flowers are pretty and good to eat. Rose petals, lavender and violets are all tasty if treated right.

- Some people use wild plants to make salads or drinks. Dandelions, for example, make a tasty tea.

Why we eat

What we eat...

Staple foods
You probably have some of these foods on most days: pasta, rice, potatoes, bread, breakfast cereals...

Fruit and vegetables
Apples, bananas, pears, cherries; broccoli, carrots and potatoes. Can you think of any more?

Meat and poultry
Beef, pork, lamb, chicken, turkey and foods made from meat, like burgers and sausages

1 to live a healthy life

Dairy foods
Milk and foods made from milk, like butter, cream, cheese and ice cream.

Seafood and fish
Food from rivers and the sea – prawns, crab, tuna, salmon, cod and plaice.

We drink all of these
Milk, fruit drinks, water. Adults also drink coffee and tea.

3 to share with friends

2 to give us energy to work and play

Safety first!

● How would you like to have some seaweed for supper? Bite a bat? Or feast on a frog? Snack on a snail? Some people just love them...

Treat new foods with caution
● If you have food allergies, some foods can make you feel unwell. Check with an adult before eating new foods.

Why is it good for me?
Starchy food

You may eat cereals for breakfast, bread for your sandwiches and rice, pasta or potatoes with your dinner. These **starchy** foods are rich in **carbohydrates**. They give you energy. They fill you up so you are no longer hungry. They are rich in **fibre**. This is good for your stomach and your intestines. It helps your body **digest** food so that you stay healthy.

◄ *Eating carbohydrates gives you energy to work and play.*

Or try this...

Delicious grains...
- couscous with carrot and raisins
- wholemeal rice with grilled peppers
- oatmeal with honey and yogurt

Perfect pasta sauces...
- ham, broccoli and mushrooms
- spinach and cheese
- prawns in tomato sauce

Good or bad?

Check it out

Go shopping with your mum and compare different breads at the bakery counter. There are brown breads, bagels and French baguettes, for example.

Bad carbohydrates

All the goodness has been taken out of white bread, rice or pasta. Eat wholemeal varieties instead. Cakes and biscuits contain carbohydrates, too, but they also contains lots of sugar so try not to eat too many!

1 eat wholemeal pasta

2 eat wholemeal bread

3 eat less cakes and biscuits, sorry!

◄ *Potatoes are good mashed, with salads or baked in their skins.*

Try these super sandwich fillings...

- grilled cherry tomatoes and cheese
- ham with sliced red peppers
- bacon, lettuce and tomatoes

Why are they good for me?
Fruits and vegetables

fruits and vegetables are crammed full of **vitamins**. Your body needs vitamins so you can grow and stay healthy. There are many different types – some are listed on page 9. Each one does a different job. Some make your gums, teeth and hair strong. Some help your eyes to see in colour and find your way around in the dark. Others also make your blood clot when you have cut yourself. Vitamins even stop you catching colds. They do this by making your blood healthy so it can fight germs and infections.

▲ Eating plenty of fresh vegetables and fruits can help your teeth and gums stay healthy.

Just amazing!

Vitamins make you look good
Eating fresh vegetables and fruits gives you a smooth skin, great fingernails, shiny, healthy hair and an excellent memory!

Or try this...

Very nice vegetable treats...
- noodle and vegetable stir-fry
- celery and carrot stick snacks
- pizza with a spinach, tomato, sweetcorn and onion topping

Important vitamins

Vitamin A – good eyesight
apricots, mangoes, melons, lettuces,
carrots, peppers, tomatoes, spinach

Vitamin B – energy
bananas, avocados, beans,
broccoli, cauliflower

Vitamin C – fights diseases
oranges, grapefruit, potatoes,
tomatoes

Vitamin K – helps blood
chicory, cauliflower, cabbages

▶ *There are so many fruits
and vegetables to
choose from. And
they're all healthy!*

When you have a baked potato, eat the skin. It has even more vitamin C than an orange.

Fresh and fruity treats...

- Enjoy wobbly jelly with fresh strawberries.
- Pile blueberries and bananas into a pancake.
- Munch a mango sliced onto a waffle
  and topped with plain yogurt.

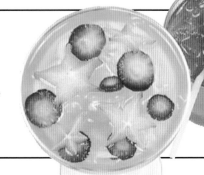

Why are they good for me?
Meats and dairy food

meat, fish, dairy foods and eggs are all packed with **proteins**. Proteins help you grow strong, tall and happy. They make and repair your body **tissues** and **organs**. Without proteins your muscles cannot grow strong. All kinds of nuts and legumes such as beans, lentils and peas are also rich in proteins.

◀ Like you, a pet dog gets its protein from meat. You, however, can also get protein from milk, eggs and legumes.

Safety first!

To get enough protein...
● **Vegetarians** do not eat meat. Many eat no fish or seafood. Some don't eat anything to do with animals, like eggs or dairy foods. They are known as vegans.
● If people cut out whole food groups – like meat, fish or dairy foods – they need to eat other types of protein. Legumes

Dairy foods

Strong and healthy

Milk and foods made from milk are called dairy foods. They include cream, yogurt and cheese. Dairy foods have lots of vitamin D and **calcium** in them. They make your bones strong and stop them breaking. They make your teeth healthy. And they give you healthy hair and fingernails.

▼ Make your burger healthier. Add lots of salad to a wholegrain bun. Leave out the mayonnaise and the ketchup.

▼ If your fingernails often break and split, you may need more calcium.

are particularly good sources of protein. Eat plenty of beans, lentils, peas, nuts, and dark-green leafy vegetables.

Are they good for me?
Fats and sugar

We need to eat some fat, because it gives us energy. Fat also keeps us warm. There are two types of fat: good fats and bad fats. In most western countries we eat too much bad fat. We also eat too much sugar in sweets, cakes and biscuits. This makes us **overweight**. It can also clog our blood vessels or cause **diabetes** and **heart disease**.

◄ *Are you tempted by candy floss? Have a piece of fruit instead!*

Or try this ...

Eat less fat...
- Go easy on the mayonnaise, ketchup and other bottled sauces.
- Don't use too much butter or cream.

- Don't eat too much junk food – burgers, fishfingers, chicken nuggets.
- Cut off the fatty bits on meat, and eat 'white' meat (chicken, turkey).

Which fat is which?

Bad fats

Eating too much animal fat is unhealthy. There are animal fats in meat and in foods that come from animals: milk, butter, cream and cheese.

Good fats

Vegetable fats are very healthy. There are good fats in olives, peanuts, avocados and brazil nuts (see page 27 about nut allergies). Oily fish also have good fats – try sardines, mackerel, tuna and anchovies.

▲ *A melted cheese pizza topping tastes great, but don't eat it too often. It is full of fat and will make you put on weight.*

When you feel like snacking on sweets...
- Munch dried apricots, pears or raisins.
- Grab a handful of mixed unsalted nuts.
- Drink a glass of freshly squeezed orange juice.

How much of each food makes...
A balanced diet?

your body needs a variety of different foods to be healthy. You should eat more of some foods than of others. The pyramid on the right shows you which foods you should eat most of. The most important food is carbohydrates so the pyramid is widest at the bottom. It is narrower at the top because you should not eat too much fat.

▼ *Eating some foods from every food group makes you grow strong and healthy.*

Quiz -?-?-?-?-?

1 A healthy lunch is...

A Eating nothing at all, so you can lose weight.

B Eating as many cakes and sweets as possible.

C Eating a wholemeal sandwich with cheese and tomato, an apple, a handful of nuts and raisins, plus drinking some fresh orange juice or water.

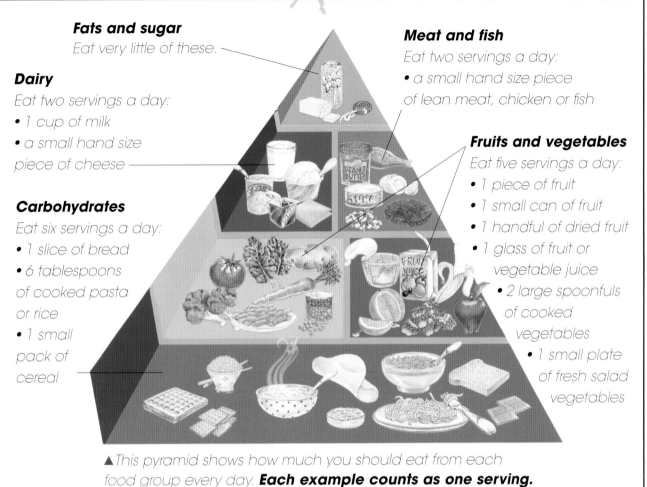

Fats and sugar
Eat very little of these.

Dairy
Eat two servings a day:
• 1 cup of milk
• a small hand size
piece of cheese

Carbohydrates
Eat six servings a day:
• 1 slice of bread
• 6 tablespoons
of cooked pasta
or rice
• 1 small
pack of
cereal

Meat and fish
Eat two servings a day:
• a small hand size piece
of lean meat, chicken or fish

Fruits and vegetables
Eat five servings a day:
• 1 piece of fruit
• 1 small can of fruit
• 1 handful of dried fruit
• 1 glass of fruit or
vegetable juice
• 2 large spoonfuls
of cooked
vegetables
• 1 small plate
of fresh salad
vegetables

▲This pyramid shows how much you should eat from each food group every day. **Each example counts as one serving.**

2 For a balanced diet it's best...
A to eat a mixture of foods from different food groups
B to eat nothing on some days
C to eat only meat and eggs

3 Most children eat...
A just the right mixture
B too many sweets
C not enough fruit and vegetables

ANSWERS: 1C, 2A, 3B and C.

15

Eating well

there's an easy-to-follow rule about eating healthy food. Try to eat 'five a day'. Not five cakes or chocolate bars, but five portions of vegetables or fruit. It's easy to do – a glass of fresh fruit juice counts as one portion, an apple or slice of melon counts as one, a selection of vegetables with your main meal might be two more servings. You only need one more: nibble on some dried apricots or peaches and you're there!

◄ *There is some truth in the old saying 'an apple a day keeps the doctor away'. Eating a variety of fruits and vegetables helps you stay healthy.*

Or try this...

To make sure you eat more fruit...
- Each time you go out to play, grab an apple or a banana.
- Snack attack? Chew on dried fruit.

- At a BBQ, fill half your plate with meat, half with vegetables.
- At a buffet, pile vegetables and salads on your plate.

Eating by colour

A rainbow of foods

Bright colours in vegetables and fruits are a good sign. They show that the foods are packed with healthy vitamins and minerals. Choose a variety of different colours.

green (good for bones and teeth): green apple, green grapes, kiwi, honeydew melon, broccoli, avocado and spinach

red (good for the heart): red apple, red grape, cherry, strawberry, red pepper, radish and tomato

white (good for the heart): banana, date, cauliflower, onion and mushroom

yellow/orange (makes you active and fresh): orange, mango, apricot, pineapple, carrot, pumpkin and squash

blue/purple (good for your memory): blueberry, blackberry, black grape, plum, aubergine and red cabbage

Just amazing!

● Not all bananas are yellow. There are more than 100 types. Some have red skin!

● Are all raspberries red? Most are red, but some are black, white or yellow.

● Eating a variety of different coloured fruits and vegetables every day protects you from some cancers, heart disease, stroke, brittle bones and other diseases.

eating...
Too much

Your body turns the food you eat into energy. Food energy is measured as **calories**. Even if you lie still in bed all day, you need to eat 1,200 calories every day. Men need to eat more than women. Active people need to eat more than inactive ones. But most of us eat many more calories than we need!

◀ *Eat too many chocolate bars and you will end up putting on weight.*

Or try this...

Are you overweight?
● If you are worried about your weight, see the school nurse. She will weigh you and give you advice if she thinks you might be overweight or **obese**.

If you are overweight or obese...
● Avoid junk food and sugary drinks.
● Turn off the television set, video games and the computer.
● Get active for 20 minutes each day.

Junk food

Which foods are junk foods?

Junk foods have very little goodness in them. They contain few vitamins. But they are high in fat, salt and sugar. They include chips, burgers, chicken nuggets, fishfingers, pizzas, many bottled sauces, crisps, sweets, chocolate bars, biscuits and ice cream. Precooked meals can also contain too much fat, salt or sugar.

How much junk food is okay?

Junk food is not good for your health. Try not to eat too much junk food, even if you like the taste of it. You will look nicer and be healthier without junk food.

Just awful!

- At least 155 million school children worldwide are overweight or obese.
- Obesity can be linked to coronary heart disease, which is now the biggest killer disease in the United Kingdom.
- As well as heart disease, being overweight can cause diabetes, strokes, cancer and other serious diseases.

eating...
Too little

many children weigh too much rather than weigh too little. But some children think it is good to be as slim as a Hollywood actor or a super model. Some think the thinner they are, the healthier they are. This is not true. The best way to stay healthy is to eat a balanced diet and take some exercise every day.

◀ *Eat healthy food, but don't skip any meals. You need to eat so your body grows and stays healthy.*

Food facts

Safety first!

If you think you are overweight...
● Ask the school nurse to weigh you. She will tell you if you really weigh too much for your age and height and will be able to give you advice about what to do.

● Do not go on a diet. Only cut out certain foods if your doctor tells you to.
● If you are worried about your size and body image, discuss it with your parents, the school nurse or the doctor.

Eating problems....

Lack of appetite

When you are ill, you probably don't feel like eating a lot. This is normal. Don't worry about it – your appetite will soon come back. Try to eat several small meals during the day. Nibble on some dried fruit. Drink a fruity milk shake.

Food dislikes

If there are some foods you do not like at all, tell your parents. Try a different food from the same group. If you don't like potatoes, try rice or noodles, for example.

Eating pains

Eating should not be painful. If it hurts to eat, you must see the doctor. They will check to see if your throat, mouth and stomach are healthy. They will help you get better quickly.

eat a variety of foods 1

eat healthy foods 2

Serious disorders!

Some people find it hard to eat anything. This is called anorexia. Others eat a lot in secret, then make themselves throw it all up. This is called bulimia. Anorexia and bulimia are dangerous eating disorders.

Anyone with an eating disorder needs to get help from a parent, a school nurse, a teacher or a doctor.

try out a new food 3

Food that can...
Make you ill

If food is not clean and safe, it can make you ill. Raw food and cooked leftovers need to be kept in the fridge. Cover them with foil and put them on different shelves. Keep the kitchen clean. Wipe up any spills. Take the rubbish out often, especially on hot days. And clear away and wash dirty dishes after your meals.

◄ *Food that has gone off can make you ill and give you a stomachache.*

Safety first!

Always be clean around food...
- Wash your hands after going to the toilet, after stroking an animal, after touching rubbish and before eating.

- Don't eat any food, like bread or jam, that has gone mouldy.
- Don't eat anything after its sell-by date.
- Keep pets out of the kitchen.

Food poisoning

Eating out and food to go

Sometimes food from a restaurant or snack bar is not very good. That could be because the kitchen is not clean or because the food itself has gone off. If you feel ill after eating in a restaurant, tell your parents. They may need to take you to see a doctor.

◀ *Always wash your hands before you eat, This is especially important if you are eating with your fingers.*

Eating too much junk food can also make you sick.

Avoid too many chips, burgers, cakes and sweets...

What to do if...

...you feel sick after eating

- Go to the bathroom to be sick.
- Afterwards, lie down to relax.
- Do not eat until you feel better.

- Drink plenty of water and fluids. Start eating again slowly – try dry toast or chicken soup.
- If it happens often, see a doctor.

How often and...
When to eat

nearly half of all children skip breakfast. Do you? After a long night without eating, it's important to have a good meal. It gives you an instant boost of all the foods you need to grow. Children who eat breakfast do better at school. Is your family rushed in the morning? Does no one have time to sit around the breakfast table? Help with tasks to get the meal ready.

◀ *A good, healthy breakfast sets you up for the whole day.*

Why is it good for me?

A good breakfast will...
- Give you more energy to play.
- Help you grow strong and healthy.
- Stop you snacking on junk food later.

- Help you concentrate at school.
- Stop you having stomachaches.
- Help you get better marks in your schoolwork.

The eating day

Breakfast

The most important meal. Eat two servings from the carbohydrate group, one from the fruit group and one from the milk group.

School lunch

Avoid fatty meat and chips. Choose fresh vegetables and fruit. Take your own packed lunch. Make it as exciting and interesting as you can.

Evening meal

Have a light meal in the evening. Eat early, then relax. Don't eat a huge meal just before you go to bed.

▲ *Put banana slices over your cereal for tasty flavour and extra vitamins.*

▶ *Try a soft-boiled egg. You can make toast 'soldiers' and dip them into it.*

Or try this...

Tasty breakfast ideas...
- strawberries or peach slices with plain yoghurt
- fresh fruit smoothies

- jam on wholemeal toast
- toasted muffins with cheese
- pancakes filled with lots of different fruits

TIDAK HALAL

Food choices

not everyone eats everything. People have different reasons for refusing some foods. They may not like the taste of a particular food. Or they may have a disease like diabetes, which means they have to be careful about the amount of sugar they eat. Some religions have rules about what food people eat and when they should eat it. Vegetarians choose not to eat any meat.

◄ *A Muslim family buys its meat from a halal butcher. Halal meat is butchered according to Muslim rules.*

Or try this...

Some vegetarian treats...
- veggie burger with cheese
- spaghetti with pumpkin and nuts
- baked potato with pinto beans

- BBQ peppers, onions and courgettes
- bean salad with eggs
- banana and mango juice
- grilled peaches with honey

▲ *Illness can also keep you from eating certain foods. Diabetics, especially, must be careful to eat a healthy, balanced diet.*

Always check that your food does not contain anything that you are allergic to.

What are allergies?

Some people get very ill when they eat a food that they are allergic to. There are different sorts of **allergies**. Some people can't have milk or milk products, others can't eat nuts or gluten (gluten is a starch in bread, biscuits, pasta and cereals).

▶ *People with nut allergies get very ill if they eat nuts. Never give nuts to little children. They might choke on them.*

Safety first!

Allergies can kill
● Never give a person with an allergy a food to eat that he or she is allergic to.

● Always read labels carefully. Allergy-causing foods are not always obvious.
● If you have a strong allergic reaction go straight to a hospital.

Look forward to...
A healthy life

find the lifestyle that is right for you. Eat more if you are very active, less if you aren't. Choose healthy foods and drinks. Eat small amounts of less healthy foods. Cut out junk food altogether. Get more active and you will have a healthy body, a lively mind and feel happy.

▲ *Living a healthy life is not boring. It gives you energy to do what you want to do.*

Safety first!

Do eat and drink...
- lots of water, fruit juice and milk
- lots of colourful fruit and vegetables
- varied foods from different groups

Don't eat or drink...
- lots of sugary drinks
- food high in salt, sugar or fat
- food mainly from one food group

Test yourself

Healthy food choices:

**1. All these are fatty foods.
Which one is healthiest?**
A a large fruit-flavour ice cream
B a bag of mixed, unsalted nuts
C a cream cake with topping

2. To eat healthily you should...
A avoid all fat
B eat only small amounts of fat, choosing vegetable fats whenever possible
C eat lots of cream

3. Which drink is healthy?
A a fresh fruit juice
B a small diet cola drink
C a large, fizzy fruit-flavour drink

Healthy lifestyle choices:

**4. If you are overweight,
you can lose weight by...**
A making sensible food choices and getting active every day
B spending three hours every day exercising in the gym
C eating nothing for a week

**5. If you don't like to eat
meat, you should...**
A try to eat it anyway
B eat lots of sweets instead
C eat a balanced diet with lots of vegetable proteins such as soya beans and legumes

ANSWERS: 1B, 2B, 3A, 4A, 5C

Food facts

eat lots of fruit and vegetables

eat wholemeal foods

avoid fats and sugars

Or try this...

● Think of fruits and vegetables starting with each letter of the alphabet – then try eating them over a few weeks.
● Try out a new fruit each week.

● Learn how to grow vegetables. Then learn how to cook them.
● Compete with friends: Who can go without sweets the longest?

Glossary
What does it mean ?

allergies: *Allergic people become ill, get rashes or breathing problems when they eat some foods or touch some things.*

calcium: *We need calcium for healthy teeth and bones. Milk and cheese contain lots of calcium.*

calories: *We measure food energy in calories. Many people eat more calories than they need.*

carbohydrates: *Starchy or sugary foods are full of carbohydrates. Carbohydrates give us energy.*

diabetes: *A diabetic cannot control the levels of sugar in her or his blood. Many diabetics are overweight, but not all.*

digest: *How your body breaks down the food that you eat.*

fibre (dietary): *Substances contained in fruit and vegetables, which help digestion.*

heart disease: *A dangerous disease. The blood vessels are blocked or narrow. It is hard work for the heart to pump blood around the body, so the heart gets ill.*

obese: *very overweight. Ask your school nurse if you think you might be obese.*

organs: *Parts of our bodies, for example heart, lungs, stomach, kidneys, ears or eyes. Each organ has a particular job.*

To find out more...

...check out these websites:
- www.bhf.org.uk
British Heart Foundation
- www.healthyfridge.org/justforkids.html
Open the fridge door to a healthy heart!

- www.healthykidschallenge.com
Activities, games, recipes, and challenges related to healthy eating.
- www.kidshealth.org
Information on healthy eating.

overweight: *too fat. Ask your school nurse if you think you might be overweight.*

proteins: *We need to eat proteins for our bodies to grow and heal. Meat, fish, dairy foods and legumes (vegetables such as beans and peas) are rich in proteins.*

starchy: *containing starch. Pasta, potatoes and rice are starchy foods.*

tissues: *Your body and its organs are made up of different tissues, such as bone.*

vegetarian: *A person who does not eat meat. Vegetarians called vegans also do not eat animal products, like butter or eggs.*

vitamins: *We need to eat tiny particles called vitamins to grow and stay healthy. Fruits and vegetables are rich in vitamins.*

To find out more...

...read these books

- Gaff, Jackie. *Why Must I Eat Healthy Food?* Cherrytree Books, 2005.
- Ganeri, Anita. *How My Body Works: Eating.* Cherrytree Books, 2006.
- King, Hazel. *Carbohydrates for a Healthy Body.* Heinemann Library, 2003.
- Powell, Jillian. *Fats for a Healthy Body.* Heinemann Library, 2003.
- Royston, Angela. *Proteins for a Healthy Body.* Heinemann Library, 2003.
- *Look After Yourself* KS2 CD Rom. Evans Publishing Group, 2006.

- www.nutrition.org.uk
The British Nutrition Foundation website. Features a special section for schools.
- www.galaxy-h.gov.uk A Department of Health website for children.

Index

Which page is it on?